HERE COME THE WARM JETS

CITY LIGHTS SPOTLIGHT SERIES NO. 10

ALLI WARREN

HERE

COME

THE

WARM

JETS

CITY LIGHTS

SAN FRANCISCO

CITY LIGHTS SPOTLIGHT
The City Lights Spotlight Series was founded in 2009,
and is edited by Garrett Caples.

The editor would like to thank Lindsey White, Maia Ipp, Jason Morris, Cedar Sigo, and
Margaret Tedesco of [2nd floor projects] for their assistance with this title.

Library of Congress Cataloging-in-Publication Data
Warren, Alli.
[Poems. Selections]
Here come the warm jets / Alli Warren.
pages cm. — (City Lights Spotlight Series ; no. 10)
"All City Lights Books are distributed to the trade by Consortium Book Sales and
Distribution"—T. p. verso.
ISBN 978-0-87286-609-6
I. Title.
PS3623.A86438H47 2013
811'.6—dc23
2013013796

All City Lights Books are distributed to the trade by
Consortium Book Sales and Distribution: www.cbsd.com

For small press poetry titles by this author and others,
visit Small Press Distribution: www.spdbooks.com

City Lights Books are published at the City Lights Bookstore,
261 Columbus Avenue, San Francisco, CA 94133
www.citylights.com

CONTENTS

ACKNOWLEDGMENTS

Thank you to the following presses for publishing chapbooks in which some of this work first appeared: Lew Galley, Editions Louis Wain, Mitzvah Chaps, and Lame House Press. Thanks also to the editors of the small magazines and journals who published versions of these poems. The poem 'Catullus 83' appeared in *The Poems of Gaius Valerius Catullus* (Krupskaya, 2011).

This book would not have been possible without the love and support of my friends and family. This book is for them.

HERE COME THE WARM JETS

ACTING OUT

You begin from economic fact
You enter in overalls, a tart talisman
      distinguished by what you do and how you go about doing it
You are a perceptible, finite and particular
      part of the scaffolding
Your personal qualities should ideally be completely irrelevant
      chains of forgetting
You arise therefore from your stomach and your imagination
You invite the little lady onstage
      and run along the nerve from the base to its point in a flat arc
You are whatever you can afford and arrange,
      wherever you can imagine to appear
You are this third thing
      fixed only in the variety of your manifestations
      a universe of meaning, value and practice
You are the vehicles through which you spread misinformation
You are sensitive and magnetic to metal
You are the clause built into the law
      significant, fungible and durable
      trolling the show me state

You await universal permission
        get baked and walk the lake
You are pushing yourself up against the wall and you are petting
        riding bitch in the benz
You are the amalgamation of your conceptions
        and their consequences
You are the structures you live by
        and act unfettered against anything
        detrimental to your interests
You are the bean eaters
        couched in productive forces
You are the humming cycle of land under your feet
        bound by the contract
        shooting up the overpass with pink paintballs
        hampered by involvement with your own subject matter
You are accused of being a lyric poet
You shadowbox ressentiment
        and swell the numbers
You are the relations of exchange by way of this accumulation
        audible in the following way
Your property is an extension of you
        set apart from all the world
Your eye, your ear, your pelt is self-serving

You are not so different as a mastiff is from a greyhound,
      a spaniel from a shepherd's dog
Your logo satellites your diaphragm
      and saturates your body
Your desire is elemental and abundant
You mutually dissolve and engender your love
      thus your mass
You are the ceaseless excess of little green things
Your engine went by at 6 o'clock, your cab went by at 9

FERTILE CORRESPONDENT

The looping points like likeness and so forth
asserts that everything happens because
I do not know how to work metal
I am less effective I devote a great part of my time
to the interpretation of signals when signs are slow
in coming I do not hesitate to seek the slightest touch
by water by wheatberry by cotton thread and flintstone
I lick around the perimeter and lick under
that other totality to overthrow with a flick of tongue
that I might run to the top of a high hill
without weariness sprout a disc and make bold claims
aim to come correct come morning
after morning in full range in weights
and looting insert fingers to bring breath

NEWSWORTHY THING

that we would have been visible from the air
that we would have acted as such
that we would return
having been forced
to have been grazing

that we were springs
and by some spell spurring
banks & batons blockading
what we could have been growing
that we would have been greeting
the horde the gregarious horde

we could be seed and carried
intact esteemed
partaking among coming
in flesh allayed
as reprieve
according there
in thrust and present

that we would be given
and pillars
and by some spell spurring
soft-bodied welling
that we could equate
with what we confiscate

great channels flowing
visible from the air
and running tides
and concrete lapping
and steel girders

that we would be wrenching
and never rest
and carry & turning
and teeth again
brooks that blood
reeking at the port entry

WHOSE RULES RELATE REGARDLESS OF THEIR NAMES

Join the group Work, Awareness of Death, & Sexual Continence

Visit the Great Dismal Swamp

Visit the Online Help Center

Become a fan of boat-like gliding

Drink the port-like wine

Poke the quadriceps

Poke the wild nettle

Become a fan of adaptability of skiffs

Make money not steel

Hear the chimes

Flourish as foci

THIS WILL BE THE MATERIAL OF MY SONG

Another day at the sieve
administering the field

& all its relations
bound in custom

to enterprise and acquire
to load into carts

Everyone wants to hang glide
in colonial paradise,

no? To stand on the brink
and make a market

of every vital nucleus
As much in understanding

as execution
of lops, tops and rootage

of dragging and gathering
With whom it is permissible

with whom it is forbidden
to rub larynx and articulators

with my habit and my uzi
and the bishop of worms

as an example
to the population

SENSORIUM

The figure must be a professional at the call of his job
This job will not wait till she has the leisure to spare for it

And so smiths and other craftspersons must share the work
And swell the numbers

The cesspool-cleaner and the ceruse-maker
They market their bodies and call the return
They get for it their wages

They produce corn, wine, clothes and shoes,
     and build themselves houses

And in whose veins
A variety of delicacies, scents, perfumes, call-girls,
     and confectionary

And we need a lot more servants—tutors, wet-nurses, nannies,
     cosmeticians, barbers, butchers and cooks
And we need swineherds too

In the summer they for the most part work unclothed and unshod
In the winter they are clothed and shod suitably

For food they serve splendid cakes and loaves and sit down to feast
       with their children
And they have wine to drink too

So they lead a peaceful healthy life, and die at a ripe old age,
       bequeathing a similar way of life to their children

And repeat the process often in the hour of the sun

And various country dishes

And what sorts of things are to be feared

To carry arms and ride

THE SQUAD AND I SKI AND SWAN

The squad and I ski and swan
Thus a prayer is a sentence
And individuals are predicated
By the eyes and face
By our being holding them
By which I mean I met
Convulsions both moving & impressive
Shall commence then & proceed
Out of several secretions
In lice, nits; in flies, grubs and fleas
Like eggs, all the like nondescripts
In the house say Ho
So too on the sea
Prey upon prey
The broads and tenants
Flock the nest to top and swarm
The nectar the squad
And I ski and swan

SOLEMN ASSEMBLY OF THE TRIBE

We meet in a ditch
an ordinary, sensuous ditch
We ride in on steel
rosy in the sugarloaf
in which bathing partakers
spread in full salute
on mallow & asphodel
The heap carries a parcel
towards that warm
entrance that protein
likewise hauls pack
across the mine out
into the open shudder
on the blooming base
The work is difficult, traceable
by the love in me
open the door
show us your teeth

A FEW FACTS ABOUT THE THORAX

Oh come, it's all over the faces of the ~~wage earners~~ figures
And seas and rivers
The occupied lands and the empty open lands
The sticky surface of everything
The pirates and captains also

Oh come, won't you believe in forgiveness?

We must sit around in sun and make sure ~~love~~ we does not escape
We must go to the coast alone
We must never go to the coast alone

It must be somewhere about Try to see
If you can catch sight of it tell me what it is

Often a part is impelled
Without the whole being impelled

Pulped, fermented and elaborated into lines

And the whole sequence of external things
On the cheek of youth

Plumb in the uprights
Braced in the beams

Oh come, won't you forgive me?

One must never go to the country

If you are in the country then I cannot lick your asshole
And everything that is throbbing and heaving and sopping
Will not throb and heave and sop

BUMMER AND LAZARUS

I read the books
of discoveries of men

their ratting talent
and unique bond

they mark the burning
with a flag

I look up to find the whole
Quarterly aglow

I name all owners
of this district

& say how much
each of them owns

wanting the interlocked grills
to splinter wooly

unpenetrated bodies
to love more wanting

a relational empire
of unabating gaze

The death of Lazarus
precedes the death of Bummer

I WAS LIVING IN A DEVIL TOWN

I was gathered into a nation
drawing reference
to circulation to signs
I was beginning to suspect
the reason being needing
to murder all this doubling
this menace
as all private parts
precede and mislead
their patrons
on a night like tonight
fortuitous and bright
conserve and remain
following the mode of error
there the off-duties holler back
I was in the camp
making function
my number one priority
my balls and my word

ALL MY ACTIVITIES ARE FEEDING ACTIVITIES

Dear Commissioner
here are my directive accounts
of genitals and cash
now bring me your goods

We don't live among fowlers
Not all poisonous juices are burning
or bitter nor is everything now
which is burning and bitter poisonous

Air is removed from the workspace
and dispersed into the multiverse
It's very strict metadata
You get echoes and dropouts

For the most part
Juliet is gaseous now
as a caucasian she gets it
on the head and face and I move
from hypocrisy to cynicism

Cristal all over the face and neck
concrete and glinting
audible light on jumbotron
marmalade for miles
That good wood kept calling my name
Behavior meet Behavior, Behavior
meat all the social organs

A PLATE OF HAM AND GOAT'S MILK

In late summer of that year
weeks were made of beating

I was in love with facts
decked out in preen oil

aided by contact with the mouth the limbs
thickening and full of peeping

in the same way as all movement carries one
in the direction of the natural is natural

the regimen must be made more moist
So I set these things down this way

and say these things are true
in the army in the navy by law

by sites of thinking and acting
with spore sacs and sac fruits

for anyone who has eyes to see
whose status is tied directly to the ability

to give pleasure
with ceruse and alkanet dye

with wings and plumage
like colts into noise

in their opulence together
with chariots the cavity is arable

MY FACTLESS AUTOBIOGRAPHY

The grammarian chooses a place in the open
air for arguments fiction runs sweet
in my nostrils I inhale
a failing air fleet
four of them for to eat
the milky crab the pudding
proof is found in

I am the Assayer of Weights and Measures
I am what I am because I am not
something else I hold a lily
in my hands it is not gross
As a fabric is a historic surface I am propelled
I touch bone & traffic in salt
like minefields & the people we inhabit

Who but the most despairing among us
will dwell on that point tonight?
Good brother, take me to the place
where I may meet ghosts and protein

Where hiatus does not interrupt
the phrasal unit and International Agencies
in which the State participates
consider a lover a stash

My freedom is represented by my desire
to twiddle beard & make face
at women in their apartment windows
I poke my snout through the underbrush
and keep a stash of guilt I unleash
when a red-face appears
When her hat flies off and out
the convertible I grab my pants
My member is being severed
My stomach is so concave
various kinds of hardships ensue

Dear Exploited and Missing Persons
I don't want to lose access
to fresh luncheon meat at a fair and low price
I have never seen the star you call the sun
I grasp bills like pebbles
and my brow? abounding grief

I would like to take this opportunity
to dig-out the sack
I has the booze she has the chronic
You heat water to a rolling placebo
till truth telling makes a terror threat
What with the dust and human remains
The ferry accidents the bombs
the fast-drying three feet of concrete
What makes this night different
from all other mauls?

At the dog park in the club
People from the valleys from the uplands
from the highest slopes betroth
This play houses countless characters
Young men will stick you up
Imagine walking around the market
not knowing what the seahorse is for

SAUSAGES, HOGSHEADS, LEGS OF MUTTON, LARD, TRIPES

and tubs of wine
in the duct again
additive and beautifully redundant

interspecific pit
of a possible world

I work hard to know
if there is any gold
My job is to mop ejaculate

I employ swim-a-phone
in high impact accessories
and make a face beneath noise

all tingly from the consommé
I roll back jersey and claim
clams I work at
collecting are lush pastels

and when you talk
I just watch your mouth

This is the day
I have to write about now
These are the ham hocks
and their unanimous consent
you've been waiting for

Tell your mom I said hi

MANUEL LOVES ROBIN

I conceived the desire
to take my pleasure dear Stacy
I wanted to put my desire to execution
I am a caring girl who loves to flip
but I really blew it
in the finals got great red spot
all over my face
got caught splayed
by the cherry picker
bobbing in the August air
calling everyone cockface
slappin ass all the ladies in the house
show me colts, stack them bones
And then I feasted
on duckbreast and roast chicken
and ale and figs and cream
I held it in my mouth
for a spell dripping jewels
all over the port town

FLIPPER TURNS TWENTY-FIVE

and it's reeking
this hood. By at least
three modes the flooding
comes. And comes
in little plastic purses, denim
and beach stone. The sea is too cold
for wading and messages
drop off. I slap your
girlfriend's ass and write
three apology emails. *Try
Magazine* comes out
every two weeks. Flipper
turns twenty-five, buys
a lady's coat and heavy duty
trash bags. The little blue envelope
slides in and out and Otis
wants you to open the door. Badly
the beat, it's incessant, this great
pollen plow. In October you go
to the sea and don't wade.

There is a special kind of goose
which thrives during this time
and throbs. Waking life. The bulb
is incessant, donk for days.

TO NEWLY COME INTO THE STATE OF A MILKER

who in earnest develops
a function-oriented model
out of skinflints and constrictions
giving dap at the rind
winded up in two substances
which is absurd
I never know what's suitable for a gift
I lack the proper chemicals to vacate
all aghast and thrashing
& in the end rejecting
while engaging
after all wanting
those little materialists
till every attribute and cavity
sway splayed
which is absurd
If you are ready at dawn then I will start
send word we are encompassed

WELL-BRED AND POST-COITAL

Went afflicted with vapors
to the armament
A political animal
an amputee derived a stitch
to prick pin with
The pricking proves
to broaden the back's capacities
to drop anchor
in a hot hay bed

I stick my tongue in
and then I stick
my finger, forearm & mouth in
I venture all around
that fly gucci
whispering to mutes
voiding my friends

What tail feathers what citizens of cities
So much ice on the watch

the law proves a gaze
gets neighbored
becomes a species

    It's not you it's
the smirk truck and dewy air
    People At Large
collect this in stacks and show it
urgers encourage

    Approach a body
a pleading face
Mark the parting
of each eye enclosed
    Here lies a constituency
    A peninsula for friends
Dictation in dark margin
Thou to the extreme
 lifted in spores

I NEED HELP WITH THIS

I like this calling bell
makes me feel this anagram bell
I bury my face in your chest
this warm jet this great need
All the gold in all the world
in a woman's ass. This poem
an object between persons
I'll hold it up higher, higher, high

THE HELP I NEED IS NOT AVAILABLE HERE

I need help with long term hope
I need help with the dawn
of war and achieving
my new year's resolutions

This praise song
and the problem of pornography
structures this praise song
as speaking placement

I need help moving my chickens
I need help with girl problem
my dog, like, keeps marking the wrong areas?

and my breasts
this most pressing issue
like choosing between best friends
a distance problem involving constant
acceleration and tethering glitches

The party's all "descendant selectors, please!"
and me I'm in my handspring visor
and my bird plucking problem

I need help with a bat script for parsing
I need help with pricing with naming this
praise song I said
I seriously need help with the whole set up ASAP!

so it's
40.08 / 100.09 (grams of molecular mass of calcium carbonate) =
moles of calcium

then
(moles of Calcium x .1973ml (convert grams to ml)) / 0.05

I got 1.580 ml
is that right?

CAN I PREVENT MY WAGES FROM BEING GARNISHED?

It was late in the evening
so you know I had something special on
for pants I was tooling around null.com
seeking the affection of the ones
to whom affection does not come easily Hi
First of all I'd like to thank throaty emphasis
for guiding this feed
to allow a stilted seller access
to insight at a reduced rate per pop
Secondly let me be fortunate enough
to meet a charming young thing
with big breathy icons and significant overlap
What's the difference between making fun and poking at?
Can my wages be garnished
if I'm a junior high school student? If my contract contains
the phrase Touch My Pleasure, Secretary General
you are forewarned and volunteering
in participating in implementing
this beautiful and fiscal thing, this work

is not strategic it serves and in serving
pursues stacks and flumes
and golden berries, arming and lifting
nice spread Thanks Hello
it's late in the evening
I'm texting the conductor

PLUS DOME

As I watch the moon wax
again tonight I'm thinking of you
Bubbles your trusses of riveted
girders. Let's start
with autobiography. There are two
distinctions I want to make
My bluebook was blank
now chiclets steady stream
all aboard daily. Thank heavens
I think it's real. Knock knock
the milkman bears reference
tracing the rim a river
of O. Pounding that foghorn
all the way to Watsonville
grape jelly in the whiffs

CATULLUS 83

WITH BRANDON BROWN

I'm sorry I said
chomping on the warm jet Mary
     instead of mapping all
religious holidays and rites of spring
into your powerbook

glued as I am
to multimodal devices & telepresence
     I failed
to merge cells swiftly
for that I'm sorry but I refuse
to be the only one
     that fatuous ass
appears exponentially bulbous
in every office park and mobile
surveillance tower
in the greater geographic area

     She's got this manner
of speaking so much with her blooming

woo that I forget
to increase the value of the world
        of things &
the ripe one gilded
in blinding cardigan sheen
        and everything
we'd been trying to prevent
by rolling around on the floor
with virtue and fealty
        slipped into silt

Just look at me now perving
on handclaps and sapsuckers
clapper rails and
        I can't really move
the light budding before me
all kinds of soft tissue
        I just want to make it
out alive boss

did you not receive my note?
as I was dealing with the goo
        a lady out for an evening stroll

was attacked by a sack of bees!
I heard screams
       instead of heroic deeds
of valor and blinking
as she blinked how I can be extra
gentle about it
       I slurped shellfish
and fell into a nap
       valves highly calcified
I mean a rendition

LET THE AIR COMB THEM

The mouth can't or won't
move from the bench
Breathing peopled cupping
coming day basting
this point from which
a whole future flows
milking the heart
of the plate after a deep drive
to centerfield
bareback on the green
It helps us run fast
throw long and hit far
We wipe each other off
It helps our hue

MY FACTLESS AUTOBIOGRAPHY

I arise around survival of the event
as worse than the event
The whole place surrounds the smell
I take one step toward and ten paces back
breathless with the mirrors
with the fees and meters
Feces I fax my demon family
weeping on the bridge again

My condition was induced as follows
Releasing actual sales numbers, trying to mount
the policeman or his horse
tonguing captains manually
strong simultaneous tendencies to approach
and avoid appearance and avoidance

Men come to my cherry doors to carry on
about finance and cricket
coaxing a cavernous oath
wrestling natives into nestling

My part is basically to hatch
with regard for human dignity and life
In my best foreign automobile
stunting the stupor fronting us

In order to love my country better
I offer monthly meter readings
I am filled with rhythm, passion and speed
protruding in public
popping my collar into a wreck

My father sits me down
Son, he says, don't let them enter
your mouth I wrote a narrative
about our collective pain
and went shopping

I LIKE THESE SPATIALLY DENSE GLADIATORS

I like the novelty
how the two ladies
how they both combined
proportions things that just appear

I like the ease of her bias
how she pairs it
taking what is considered
maybe more ridiculous
with her gray shift

and I'm just looking
I don't have fur on me
I like paintings and whatever
the idea of something classic

Also I like color
how they look as a group
I like her small hat
the wing-y aspects

I like Mami's topknot
I used to live there

I like the idea
her cute empire
to intertwine the two
that they both have shoes
I like it as dirty though

I like a lot now
and her injection
how she keeps it
her sweet white locket
how you glint

SOME GREATER SOCIAL SHARING

with two eyes fixed
on one profile

doing the pre-
emptive poke

fetching and carrying
cake as functionaries

in hay
in which we are

seized only later
on in perpetuity

we do this daily
we sink our teats

in sauce
there's very little

one can say exactly
except to point

in parting what
one does is blink

GETTING READY TO HAVE BEEN FULLY ENSCONCED

I touch the work
the work touches me

the backdrop is a fine mesh
through which posses thump and leak

icing emerging markets
in which the gathering mound protrudes

This the grammar
in which form comes

This the nature of the transcript
between persons

that terminal moraine
ever attenuating from lap to lap

Sometimes foghorns reach city-centre
Sometimes one hundred spondees provide the tools necessary

to utilize a system while maintaining
a case concept not bound by that system

And that is the story
of how I earned my purple heart

Balled up on the murphy bed
accusing nipples of gold digging

lacking the conviction necessary to move
off the unconfused upholstery

Getting ready to have been fully ensconced
They tell you what you need is intake packets

but I want to tap the gap back
till form and form's fiancé turn fatback

I've been down with men's frank tearfulness after epic victories
I've known a diverted thrust or two

That plump lushness
bending the bits

Dear impresario, do it
where the congress can't reach us

AS A SIGNAL TO RISE

Often I am compelled
to develop a fleet
of swarms and shoals and eager
clients to flourish in the first
in assistance of freeboaters
& establishment of bases

I ask fates for their consent
let us be undone
by coming array
let the conflicted and anxious
the seed-savers and hard-hearts
the gulls and mussels and shrimps
let them with ears hear

all waters we call our sea
and peoples we include in this we
whether compatriot or foreigner
whether felled by axmen
or suspended in exception

bodies break on the wheel
for verse to take the place
of differentiated plunder

Often I am permitted
on damp docks
to show the excess of it
& you see me kind of grinning
precisely because I am a fiddler
believe me sweetie
I got enough to feed the needy

COCO WAS A ROYAL

in the heart of the enormous capital
Americans are not ashamed

A lady holds a balance
which appears less to have been raised

than erected in greeting
load-borne and load-bearing

The way I got the job was
humility in justice and sufferability (Ibid.)

The crime is not cute
The crime is horrendous

My own fetching fidelity my dog's also
I smooth it on a partisan cupcake

pestilent at the after-party
in the heart of the enormous conglomerate

scars speak back
hillocks against the horizon

We drink dulled wine in warm tubs
& do the dipsy twostep

Bone suckers, bean eaters
they lap up the exhaust

BRASS HATS

Coming day beaming
prance prance devolution
"showing itself as a self-
sent herald" an exact
replica of the billboard
proclaiming coming naught
what a buncha vegan mess on the night shift
federation of melancholy machinists
moist at the arbitration proceedings
corking mink in mudroom
finger on the cowbell unawares
For I am vested
for my sins
my capacity to turn
the living to dead
a collective phenomenon
suffered individually
on account of the unkempt
case of my bodily
part in watery alliance

with flipping and spreading
& enjoining without ever being
satiated or easy-going
Call me Ho-Ho
collapse is inscribed
you in your linen robe
me in my silvery cloak
all the statues of the city
decked out in stocking caps
the President waves
the Jeweler also waves
Pretty Ricky
Seimone Augustus
& swoop in particular
"as water loves air"
eagerly among the ambiguous
logo tatted on my going away part
no extra charge for the stinger

PLOW POSE

I feel like it's a matter of economics
this rotgut wine
and bad lilt
it takes an industry of
experts, spreaders
their dual-purpose
for tillage and for trade
packing on the path
carting on the plain
Who will account for
the kingdom is interested
in crossed high spears
that's the second time this week
my mouth's mouth
by turns inflated & empty
yanked on the latch to say
in the ether and the air
in fire that produces things
the fairly specific things
you do with the left hand

yawning and starting to rub
in the dark middle
in what is wet
in circulation
from a single satellite
how I hold it up as firmament
of joining through distortion
bread is plentiful
and life unstrenuous
in bright array
honeycomb in the drone

MAMMALIAN DIVING REFLEX

Swamp-face & I find the finer things
distasteful   yak weave, chicken bloom
Oyster Perpetual 940L
        charting the dobby loom
Look at the swim
thick with lesser scaup
heaving what The Party exudes
        Burberry, Democracy
standing or sitting or whatever

From the rooftops you see
the limbs of the city
where we do not venture
& those that are off limits
according to caste
        Where peep tom & ghost face
prepare their masonry groove
        Allied on the atoll
taken to the count
asked to account for his lack

of active concern
with the nastyass honey badger
and proper charging procedures

I am overwhelmed
in the office park, Santi
in the kingdom of records
in which the ends are people
according to tax
All those with septa intact
prep with lemongrass, purslane
moss-rock of the San Lorenzo
beading what the struck clock's not
Cling persist, lamby
lend ear to the ordinance
of the guilds
Not of magnitude but of ways

ENVIRONMENTS FOR SHOPPING

conquered in a car seat
rite of passage PTSD
with my bowl cut & my bright green NLG cap
compelled to comport
looting largely locally
I press painted marks
against men as they shake
their spears police the periphery
and bully them all
who gather firewood in forests
and fish undrained fens

I saw a goat
commuting across the plain
a fiscal functionary
in the governed provinces
an orange grove in the mall

Hello from this nasty canopy
this mossy pink welcome mat

What's a crabtree anyway
what's an actually existing socialism
does a pup not crave ativan in the flatlands?
does wealth not stink up the sidewalks there?

The barracoon the jail the crimp house
the suburb the slum the supermax slammer
we dance in a circle around the debris
to make real the horrors of accumulation
and go off content with the little party

A PRACTICE KNOWN AS CHURNING

I went to the city some days
to learn my master's pleasure
& laid fort at the farthest place
where hedges are highest
& terror of the obvious
is a rosary of similitude

Did you see some of the nudging?
How did you feel about the nudging?

Boats by water and wagons by land
in active assistance in perpetuating
fraudulent froth & hence
with haste I've seen
their mulchy tongues
suck up every animate aim
sweeping excess into piles

the reserves and neocons
administrators and representatives

the preachers and deputies
and yahoos and spodies
In the evenings they come down
from their operational sectors
to kiss the children

what terror is in them
to keep the sugar boiling
to restrain the wanderings
as fragile and fictitious

Did you see the tent on a stick?
Did you see the architecture of gathering?

I go to the city some days
to gather what's left of scrubgrass
There in the alley we converse
Idris his love of fresh skim
Ted his disdain for women
their lack of banking
Terrence and Will their concern
for purity of pussy

power precedes them
sap-drenched
& parceled
across the land

I go to the city some days I receive a letter
Dear Comrades
don't get it twisted
never lick the hand that lashes you
use beef when you run out of oakum

HIDE THE POOR

As clansmen make laws
the country makes heaps
kings and governors
proclaim franking
to be among inalienable rights

They burn youths
with warm wooden pipes
to leech bread from them
to flood the grazing land
to be brought to experience

The painter deemed most skillful
is asked to depict this
without adulteration
with just one remaining ventricle

Wherever he ventures clerks
give him honor

and cooked food
because they like his commodities

some beads
and little bells

and reciprocally
and how

The unimaginable
deemed inevitable

Prophecy is memory
& our fate is extraordinary

especially in the mines
but not only there
I'm trying to arrange feathers
on this ceremonial shield?
this idea of coinage?

I'm trying to bring meat
heads and steel and crafts

to the gospel of justice
I'm delighting in the bursting
of asset bubbles

Not being subjects
they have no desire
No love for moms

Can't you hear that reeking?
Don't you see the big chain
Don't you see the big grill
Call that deflection
in place of action
Send a banger
crying through the streets

SOAP ROCK

In those days men had to have
a memory for many things
to drive off wind and favor
the seed a narrow belt of springs
cast across the heart of the land
and light like glass
To set oneself up in white
in this fever-ridden valley
beyond all wavecrash
where it is still possible
to dine today to bear boasts
from a firm sedan chair
with a bung at the back
laid out under oak
for love of returning
to the source
wine, lavender, women
of easy virtue
she looks good when you row
Come, know the privilege

of distilling it
the cooling tube of the still
cold meat & oat cake
jawnz domestic and official
yield up the breast and sing
and do not blush for it
Bring my ghost a calvados

JUNK IN THE TRUNK

this locket
on the ring I'm holding
keeps coming unhinged

I only wanted to say a few words
to you slumping there
about pirates and booty
but got rubbernecked
by the ad assault
and attempts at agency
in the great green air

I only wanted your purple sails
and fanning nymphs
to garnish every hood
with a gleaming grape
To share this junk with a swath
twiddle the law
go diving in the trunk

but I just live in Woodland Hills and wilt
what a loot
limping around the articulator
clanking through the murk

Do you know how to jerk?
You hold your organ in one hand
and with the other
rock to the right & left
while progressively getting lower
and twisting your legs
in the great green air

See how I wrap around the spittoon?
it's a congealed plate
of disaffection
sucking on it
till I'm numb
Your winnings, sir

LET THEM RUN IN COTTON

Sonic, I'm a sensualist
sneaking a double hopped
in face of the brouhaha
without any inner vessel
I say let them run in cotton
in two canes and a hairbra
lest we forget
the elasticity of hostility
the monogamous habits
of anthropoid apes

I see that Finnish motherfucker
Shoeless Big Country
shameless in a tree hut
eager to dapple that poor soup girl
Sleepy Butterbean
to name his cattle likewise
but the advent's the wake
of the demise, Sonic
I want to rub along

flap folds to be set down
among The Dreamers
The Flying Housewife
The Excellent Dude
Old Bootnose

as a means to appear
fixed as Douglas-fir
elective, hypothetical, en croute
credit where desire's been
cavorting with sniveling brokers
nestled between two lips of a wound

So I refresh the window, right?
part a mouth with Mastercard
Zoloft, poll my friends
on the relative heft
of a Brazilian blowout
and turn three fingers in Meadowlark
turn and ask to be turned in turn

FARMER GOES TO THE POKEY

"whitney houston athens burning"
is your boyfriend as wasted as mine?
thru which my subjectivity is enunciated
in the multifunctional administrative city
twenty igloos and a trading post
the reed people, the selfish herdsmen
standing motionless against the melee
enchanted by ruins sometimes
there's free leftover cake
to bid an ear to multiplicity
as one is compelled, deprived
of what might multiply desire
peat moors on the Penine hills
the draining of the marshes
uncalled helmet to helmet
on the sack of Smith
Sui Sin Far is my CNN
one machine serves another
wherever the regime is laxest
collapse is pregnant

O degenerate utopia
unstoppable great green egg
help me with this nebulizer
break the squire's gates
people have the right
to put a car in a bra
the Igbo have no king

THREE BANQUETS FOR A QUEEN

where sky is pink near the lake
a hooded woman carries a dog
a baby its ear flapping in the breeze
this dog is the way I know
there is a breeze
and it does not cease
that tellers are truth-seekers
& kiddies gonna yodel
Do you know how
these birds get to eat?

At a party back in o8
the large hats of females provoked me
A tool presupposes
on the part of the one
who makes it knowledge
of its purpose
They ask me for my govt. name
They'll have me back

behind the bar in no time
kale & beans, kale & beans

I mourn the loss of the Yahoo! billboard
I link my excitement to an image
burned in a pit
is that a wreath or coat of arms?
For as long as possible
one should not blink
I have lost my touch with eggs
and the gallant men
who flew them
Stokely Carmichael
crosses his legs

OUR TENDER URBAN CORE

with lust for growing lust

I sit down as you

stand up in a gesture named "giving up"

what do they mean "the coastal areas"?

everything we want

and do not know how to need

& so I was the one who burned down the house

sullied your copy of *Republic*

Eyjafjallajökull in-a-trance

lunching an extra 15 minutes

really bold with it

Paul, love turns to mechanical currency

& all those feeeeelings

a showcase of empty meaning

take it outside & beat it with a stick

strike our tender urban sore

SINGLE IN THE TOWNS

Easter Sunday Wall of Shame
yoked pooling
in the ear, slopping
either end bobbing
for sacrament in natural fact
I call the eggs innocent
but mean pliable
Stylized by inquisitors
back bitten in the stateroom
still I'll gladly let the meat snake
for one quick pile
atop the long-haul
to bear witness
in gold & milk

and when I wake
a quibbling cabinetmaker
lodged under shadow
of what they did call
glueshut

I'll eat of loaves
lay head on the hissing track
and make a model of the contour
That "each could outlast me"
Fork-carriers
wall-leaners
they too have mothers
who arise avowed
wholesome and hyphy

THREE OUT OF FIVE WHIPS

A lot of good eateries
open for honkies
You look out on the estuary
and it is gross
full of sentiment
did she suck it or did
you just bang her
Dear Valentine
I submit my questions
to the golden tail of
what is this, a hawk?
I go to work
tides unattended
yakitori blushing

Dear Immobilizing Boot
what's the best way
to rev your whip
To fearlessly act as if
the market has a heart

To go feasting and banquet
on human possibility, fontanels
some thickening ash
in the banquette with E-40
with landline affections
this worm-fed bird
a morsel for maintains
How did it get so big & round?
I might be spreading

VOCATION & INDUSTRY

Smacking the board
Face full of fronts
To get out from under
The cult of personality
Commas, those fuckers, ruin everything
Patience, understanding, even
Vera's cracking croon
We shall have to bleed her
That'll be a dollar for the cup of milk
& a free glob of hot exhaust
For the little lady
Give me the names of several good accountants
Fix firmly the existing
Pivot point
Cut up the back of her nightgown
& keep the nameless little gremlins in a tote
Please to call it a wound, sir, and not a scar

I call Mark daily
He has no information

We build a relationship

Between the if and when

The stain or meaning

But not both

Zipper told me come

Niner told me stay

The King is people

& the cops is cantering

According to the arc of succumbing

Biting the pillow

Repatriates the body

The meaty curve

Warms as you chew

No more queasy mistresses

No more flapping red birds

Get your wallet out, it's egg cream time

Saga go viral

Saga go dumb

Alpha Beta bumps Young Turks

Weepy bloom kaput

LEFT COAST LIFTER

They said it was the loveboat
or several bars of camwood
so I pawn unwrought ingots
and knock back sarsaparilla
upon your return from the frontier
which results I need hardly relate

For most it's something of a hinterland
ineffective larder
crying-up what should be
put down, bent back
in underbrush
tonguing hole
to let a little light in
I can't feel my face
the lake's done
been dry the sun up
and took it

Those rocks we offer
as marks of the real
flap flaccidly
The hill we climbed
covered in mud
& that fine institution
Albany Hill Gas
Black Kold Madina
is an inspiration, Mbube men's singing
is an inspiration

One last swallow
dips its wings
Do swallows have wings?
Brent says this may not be the end
but when the end does come
it will certainly feel like this

PERSONAL POEM

They say the public sphere has ended
      they say caravans impede the valleys
When you're wet & stuck from last night
      don't compose a text. If you want more of what makes you
      feel, go to the market
Open your mouth say what you think you might mean
Your skin is interesting to the extent it allows you to walk into
      this bar
That pink thing covers the tits or sits in your pants
      holding you in place
      "your body is already here for you"
Stretch the way an ape does
Dead rat near the rain drain
You don't have any kids you don't even have a bathtub you have a
      stand up shower in a studio by the lake
Wash your hair once or twice a week, don't use a brush
Learn to wear contacts, drive stick
Ask for more money if they'll give it to you
      but don't mind so much
      you might die but you could end up alone & wobbly at 90

Help your great aunt with her frozen meal, kiss your grandmother
       even if she doesn't know who you are
Be kind towards the paintings of the past, remember seasons
       change your mood change the trees
Don't cancel on a friend more than once they'll feel demeaned
       Len Bias died of cardiac arrhythmia
       induced by a cocaine overdose
       the greatest player never to play in the NBA

Keep in touch with your friends
Keep a few trinkets in your wallet to balance out the plastic
Ask your brother for some things, but not advice
If you are too beautiful to be a poet, do not despair
       you are beautiful and god loves you
Keep a few bad jokes in your back pocket
       along with a notepad and flask it might get you laid
If you find your doppelganger, do not despair
When marching or dancing around fire or fucking
Don't mind a little looping
       but if there's no lily there's a problem
The Diggers radicalized the commons
Is the lesson to not exercise. Is it disgusting to eat fish & chips
He called it the Montana Goodbye

Yellow diamonds in the light
Greyhound, greyhound, greyhound, sleep

If when you wake you can't stand
       to walk around with yr eyes and coffee doesn't help
       take a nap you might wake up distinct
Spring training is over. A boat trip to some brewery
       on the other side. Said I'd never drink again
We are asked to imagine a multiplicity
       of phallus receptacles & the mental health of human beings
"Agriculture may have been a mistake"
Yoga won't help
The buildings around the city center throb
Paul Thek's American audience, smashed blueberry pint
Food to keep you alive
If you find yourself clawing around the apartment
Lace up your boots slowly, count the eyelets
       you can see the fireworks out in the harbor
       if you climb to the roof and know what a harbor is
Fitzgerald by William Bunge, Queen Mab by Percy Shelley
Cats Cats Cats, death

Your Toyota Matrix will be used against you

A wife won't be paid for the strain on her body
        carrying around a womb
The strained rib, inhibiting your capacity
A case of the schizos, the thorazine shuffle
"I'm an emerging mid-career artist"
Go to army base, go to the abandoned office park
Go to the track bet on the horses with the right names
        ignore your fear of the line of empty stalls
Try to teach your lover to drive a car if your lover does not know
        how to drive a car
Assume the wound, disregard calls for rigor
When pressed for a tale tell the one about the couch cushion almost
        burning up a house full of poets
Clean the top of the refrigerator
Read Lefebvre's 500 page book on the Commune
        ("first, translate the French")(first, learn French)
There has never been a general strike
Give some money for the crop failures give some money for the
        habitat of non-kings

Remember the hoarders, don't have too many cats
Look at the moon
When your niece pulls candles and bunnies from wall sockets

believe her she's a living relic
When he uses the word "seminal" dismiss the phrase not the name
Consult the advice columns
Your friends are not your enemies
The dream with your head magnetic to the floor
      your inability to stand up
      build a program platform for culling the names
      "One would cease to exist."
Greet the shopkeepers (first, find the shopkeepers)
      remember the name of the carpenter who built you a
      shelf is it Roger or Robert
Forgive the mice forgive the flies
Remember the debt you're living off remember being exchanged
      for a few donkeys remember how bricks get made
Treat the detritus around you as a talisman the permeable wreck
      don't claim to know what modernity is
If your date uses the word "dialectics" don't get up and walk out but
      remember this moment it's important
At the height of your priestly powers
      don't drink beer
Astrology is real
John C. Reilly plays the frumpy husband

The enormous inflatable cylinder they're building if you straddle it
        you'll wind up diseased and emotional
Remember the midwives the witches the mothers
If you lack confidence in your poetry don't compensate with
        clothes
If your son buys a box of sturdy locks and a primitive weapon
Don't talk politics with your brother he cannot be convinced
        eat dinner poetry won't sustain you what is a woman
Get it from behind
Learn to spell medieval
Be kind we must overthrow the government we are too tired to be
        kind build an underground flood build the camp your body
A full time profession in crossing legs
        one across the other then the next
        place your palm firmly against yr thigh
        keep the nerves down
Watch Vertigo with 3000 friends watch the three-screen tribute to
        conquest and empire read more history
Burn the Olympic village burn the box stores
Celebrate the birthdays of your friends and the holy holidays even
        if you're not a believer learn the tales eat the eggs
        the joy of a child with a chocolate mouth
& the sun setting

& the sun setting

      those men in Tulsa were racist despicable and wounded men
Don't have a husband
Don't go to Las Vegas even the old one go to the desert consider
      the DEA and the department of agriculture expect blockades
Mercury Retrograde will end
      but not Columbus
An artist with his boulder, men with their wide-leg stance
Try to think what a generation might mean, and epochs, but don't
      believe them, visit your friends on the reservations
      visit your friends in jail
Cultivate crushes and houseplants but not too many
Call your mother on Good Friday
Drink in the sun every once in a while
      especially if there's a slippery rock in the San Lorenzo
Translate your sadness to anger then be done with it
      everyone knows you're no good at staying mad
Decorate your loved ones with green garlands
      touch the mosses know the names of vegetation
The acts of parliament the elimination of holydays
      one should not rise before the first light
The people resisted the repressions

Dancing and frisking together
        the little titties of Abel Gance's dance number
"it's important that you be luminous"

Don't talk too much about language in mixed company
Willful memory forget everything don't doubt
Hold it where it hurts
Boys don't know colors but they call them master painters
The first person to use hoodie in a poem
It's great to walk thru the threshold quit the shaking ask for a kiss
Wear opal proud wear it with your pants
Go to the ocean
Don't keep your categories straight
Baylor, Kentucky, Chavez Ravine
They call it One Big Man One Big Truck
        but I've seen a thousand of those trucks
Don't trust the weatherman
He's no fire hydrant spinner cap oracle
They may make a robot but she'll never be Nina Simone
Thick socks, open heart
Love the tiniest ways
        out of the sidewalks into the trees
        lust before dishonor

ABOUT THE AUTHOR

Alli Warren was born in Los Angeles and raised in the San Fernando Valley. Since 2005, she has lived in the San Francisco Bay Area. The author of many chapbooks, including *Grindin'*, *Acting Out*, *Well-Meaning White Girl*, and *Cousins*, she formerly co-curated The (New) Reading Series at 21 Grand, has contributed to SFMOMA's Open Space, and presently co-edits the Poetic Labor Project.

The state of the world calls out for poetry
to save it. LAWRENCE FERLINGHETTI

CITY LIGHTS SPOTLIGHT SHINES A LIGHT ON THE WEALTH
OF INNOVATIVE AMERICAN POETRY BEING WRITTEN TODAY.
WE PUBLISH ACCOMPLISHED FIGURES KNOWN IN THE
POETRY COMMUNITY AS WELL AS YOUNG EMERGING POETS,
USING THE CULTURAL VISIBILITY OF CITY LIGHTS TO BRING
THEIR WORK TO A WIDER AUDIENCE. IN DOING SO, WE ALSO
HOPE TO DRAW ATTENTION TO THOSE SMALL PRESSES
PUBLISHING SUCH AUTHORS. WITH CITY LIGHTS SPOTLIGHT,
WE WILL MAINTAIN OUR STANDARD OF INNOVATION AND
INCLUSIVENESS BY PUBLISHING HIGHLY ORIGINAL POETRY
FROM ACROSS THE CULTURAL SPECTRUM, REFLECTING
OUR LONGSTANDING COMMITMENT TO THIS MOST
ANCIENT AND STUBBORNLY ENDURING FORM OF ART.

CITY LIGHTS SPOTLIGHT

1

Norma Cole, *Where Shadows Will:*
Selected Poems 1988-2008

2

Anselm Berrigan, *Free Cell*

3

Andrew Joron, *Trance Archive:*
New and Selected Poems

4

Cedar Sigo, *Stranger in Town*

5

Will Alexander, *Compression & Purity*

6

Micah Ballard, *Waifs and Strays*

7

Julian Talamantez Brolaski, *Advice for Lovers*